MW01169787

1

The Divine Companion

By James Allen

Contents

Foreword

It cannot be said of this book that James Allen wrote it at any particular time or in any one year, for he was engaged in it over many years and those who have eyes to see and hearts to understand will find in its pages the spiritual history of his life. It was his own wish that The Divine Companion should be the last MS of his to be published. " It is the story of my soul," he said, " and should be read last of all my books, so that the student may understand and find my message in its pages. Therefore hold it back until you have published everything else." There remain now only his dramatic works and a few poems to be included in the next edition of **Poems of Peace**. That **The Divine Companion** will prove a companion indeed to thousands who have read his books in the past, I have no doubt. To read it is to hear again the voice of tne writer, and to study its message is to once again sit at his feet. He trod the Way himself - every bit of it, and he therefore speaks as one having authority. Lovers of James Allen's works will indeed be filled with joy to know that there is yet another book from his inspired pen, and will eagerly welcome **The Divine Companion**.

LILY L. ALLEN

Part I: The Divine Companion

I, the Spirit of Truth
Am the Friend of the forsaken and the Companion of the wise,
I restore the one, and I gladden the other, and all men I protect,
though they know me not.

The Divine Companion

Truth as Awakener

1

REJOICE ! for the Morning has dawned :
The Truth has awakened us ;
We have opened our eyes and, the dark night of error is no more.
Long have we slept in matter and Sensation ;
Long did we struggle in the painful nightmare of evil;
But now we are awake in Spirit and Truth:
We have found the Good, and the struggle with evil is ended:
We slept, yet knew not that we slept:
We suffered, yet knew not why we suffered:
We were troubled in our dreaming, yet none could awake us, for
all were dreaming like ourselves ;
Then there came a pause in our dreaming ;
Our sleep was stayed ;
Truth spoke to us, and we heard ;
And lo ! we opened our eyes, and saw.
We slumbered and saw not;
We slept and knew not;
But now we are awake and see;
Yea, we know we are awake because we have seen Holiness, and
we love sin no more;
We have beheld Truth, and error has ceased to attract us.
Yea, we have seen the Truth !
Not as a dream in the night, but as a Reality with our awakened
eyes ;
As a beautiful land afar have we seen it,
And we shall press forward until we reach and possess it.
How beautiful is Truth !
How glorious is the Realm of Reality !
How Ineffable is the bliss of Holiness !
We have abandoned error for truth, and illusion for Reality.
We have turned our backs on error and confusion,
And have set our faces towards the harmony of Justice and Truth.

2

To sin is to dream,
And to love sin is to love darkness.

The awakened do not prefer dreaming to intelligent action ;
They do not choose darkness rather than light.
They who love darkness are involved in the darkness;
They have not yet seen the light.
He who has seen the light does not choose to walk in darkness.
To see the Truth is to love it, and in comparison error has no beauty,
The dreamer is now in pleasure, now in pain ;
This hour in confidence, the next in fear.
He is without stability and has no abiding refuge.
When the monsters of remorse and retribution pursue him, whither can he fly ?
There is no place of safety unless he awake.
Let the dreamer struggle with his dream ;
Let him strive to realise the illusory nature of all self-seeking desire,
And lo! he will open his spiritual eyes upon the world of Light and Truth;
He will awake, and will see all things in their right relations and true proportions ;
He will be happy, sane, and peaceful seeing things as they are.
Truth is the light of universe, the day of the mind ;
In it there is no error, no anguish, and no fear.
He who has awakened into the light of day is no more burdened with the troubles of his dreams.
They are remembered as dreams only as illusions that are dispelled.
The unawakened one knows neither waking nor dreaming;
He is in confusion, he knows not himself;
Neither knows he others, and his judgment is without knowledge.
The awakened one knows both waking and dreaming;
He is established in wisdom;
Knowing himself, he knows others, and he judges with knowledge.
He is the understander, the knower of hearts,
And, walking in the light of Truth, he knows that every dreamer will at last awake.

3

Truth awakens us out of the slumber of ignorance,
Out of the deep sleep of sin.
It calls, and they who hear and awake, become wise and blessed.
Truth appears to men, and they see it not.
It calls to them, and they hear not.
It speaks to them through their actions,
It cries aloud to them in their sufferings,
It shines upon them in all their ways,
But they hear not, neither do they see,
For their ears are deaf in slumber, and their eyes are holden with sleep.
Truth is manifest in the actions of the wise,
Its light illuminates their precepts,
But the sleeper in error has no eyes for the manifest,
And the light of Truth, falling upon his
sleeping lids, calls forth no visual response.
Where there is no understanding, the repetition of precepts is vain.
Right comprehension is needed.
The sinless mind is the seeing mind.
He who has right comprehension interprets the divine precepts by the light of his own spotless deeds.
He does not repeat in error, but understands by the Spirit of Truth.
And this is the Spirit of Truth,–
To be free from sin to abide in good deeds, and to live in peace with all.
They that do evil, know not the Truth.
The Truth is in them that do good.
The deeds of Truth shine like the stars at night, dispelling darkness.
Truth reveals the everlasting Good;
It turns night to day, and changes the appearance of all things,
So that sin and sorrow are not, and evil is no more.

4

We are awake, and see !
And we know we are awake because we see Good.
And we know we are of the Spirit of Good because our lusts have departed from us,

And the bondage of hatred is broken. We are wedded to purity;
We have put on the Raiment of Righteousness,
And we serve the Spirit of Love;
Therefore are we awake ;
Therefore we know that truth has roused us from the sleep of evil.
We are free and happy because we walk in the Light.
And we see all things clearly in that Light ;
And we know the way we walk and whither we go.
But when our lusts affrighted us and hatred enchained us ;
When darkness enfolded us, and the dream of evil held us,
Then were we bound and miserable ;
We saw only our fitful dreams ;
We knew not the way we walked, nor whither we went.
He that hates men as evil is in sin,
And he that is in sin is unawakened.
The awakened one is the lover of all men, and there is no hatred in him,
And this is the sign that he has awakened in the Truth—
That he loves them that hate him.
Truth ends the dream of evil ;
It dispels the illusions of hatred ;
It liberates the sleeper from darkness and dreams.
Awake, Ye that sleep in error !
Rouse yourselves, Ye that dream in sin !
The splendour of a higher life is round about you,
Even the life of Good. Open your eyes, and see.
Be alert, and listen that ye may hear the call of Truth,
Even the Voice of the Great Awakener.

Truth as Consoler

1

THE knowledge of Truth is an abiding consolation.
When all else fails, the Truth does not fail.
When a heart is desolate, and the world affords no shelter,
Truth provides a peaceful refuge and a quiet rest.
The cares of life are many, and its path is beset with difficulties;

But Truth is greater than care, and is uperior to all difficulties.
Truth lightens our burdens ; It lights up our pathway with the radiance
of joy. Loved ones pass away, friends fail, and possessions disappear.
Where then is the voice of comfort ?
Where is the whisper of consolation ?
Truth is the Comforter of the comfortless,
and the Consoler of them that are deserted.
Truth does not pass away, nor fail, nor disappear.
Truth bestows the consolation of abiding peace.
Troubles come to all.
Even the wise cannot escape them.
But the wise have a sure and safe refuge in the Eternal Good.
They have a Comforter, even Truth,
Who removes the sting from affliction, and disperses the clouds of trouble.
Night descends upon the pure as upon the impure ;
But it holds no terrors for the pure,
For the Light of Truth shines in the darkness with assuring radiance.
Sweet is the sleep of the innocent.
And they that rest upon the bosom of Truth repose in peace.
Day lights up the way both of the wise and the foolish ;
But the foolish are enveloped with the darkness of error,
They stumble and are bruised, and have no comforter.
But the wise walk in the Light of Truth ;
And should they stumble they are lifted up ;
Lo! they are healed and comforted.
They that have the knowledge of Truth have the satisfaction of peace.
They are not immune from the vicissitudes of life ;
They are not released from the cares and responsibilities of worldly duties;
They are not unassailed by external foes;
But they are restful at heart;
Their minds abide in the Great Calm.

2

The worldly - minded have no comforter;
But if they forsake the world, and fly to Truth,
They will receive the sweet gift of Consolation
The world is the place of pleasure and pain;
The Truth is the abode of joy and peace.
They that relinguish the excitements and dissatisfactions of the world for the sake of Truth,
Will find an unfailing Companion and Friend, even the Eternal.
Distress is in the world.
Yea, grief and sorrow abound.
But the Truth is calm;
It allays grief, and soothes away all sorrow.
Hear ye the lamentations of the world !
Wilder are they than the tempest ;
Deeper than the ocean's roar.
Truth alone can still the tempests of passion and the storms of grief.
Come ye up into the Calm.
Resort ye to the Great Silence.
Men are. swept along by the force of turbulent passions ;
But when, sorrow arrests them they cry out in anguish.
Love of worldly pleasure has brought them low, and the world can offer them no comfort.
The world distresses, but the Truth consoles.
They whom the world has destroyed and deserted,
Who are cast down by pain and sorrow,
Even they are befriended by the Truth when they turn to Truth.
None are despised by Truth;
None are turned away ;
None are left comfortless.
Ye that are weary with pleasure-seeking;
Ye that are pain-stricken;
Ye that are lonely and desolate—
Come ye to the Truth.
The Truth is above pleasure and pain.
Be ye lifted up ;
Be ye rested ;
Be ye healed ;
Be ye befriended and comforted.

3

He who clings to his delusions, loving self and sin,
He cannot find the Truth,
Cannot receive the consolation of Truth.
All that demeans and defiles must be abandoned.
Truth is not found if the love of self is not renounced.
They who lie or deceive ;
Who hate or envy ;
Who lust or covet;
Who think only of their own pleasure;
Whose aims are for self and the glory of self in all that they do,–
From such Truth is hidden by a veil of darkness,
Even they thick veil of error;
From such the consolation of Truth is withheld because they seek
for self only, and not for Truth.
They who are truthful and sincere;
Who love men and rejoice in their success ;
Who are pure and generous;
Who seek the good of others in all that they do,–
To them Truth is revealed;
Such stand face to face with Good, and receive the consolation of
Truth.
The foolish seek satisfaction in sensual pleasures;
The vain are pleased with the flatteries of the world;
The one leads to misery and emptiness;
The other to disappointment and humiliation.
The wise abide in the joy of Truth;
And there are no pitfalls for the humble,
Their feet are steadfast in the way of peace.
We have cancelled our compact with the world.
Its pleasures are put away, abandoned, renounced.
We perform the necessary uses of the world, but we no longer rest
upon its forms,
No more seek satisfaction in its thirsty desires.
Our hearts are set upon the good of all.
Thus have we found the abiding sweetness of religion.
We have found a quiet trust and a patient happiness.
We have resorted to the Faithful One, the everpresent Comforter,

Even the Spirit of Holiness.
We have taken shelter in His high Abode.
And no temptation shall draw us back into the tempestuous ways of the world,
For our refuge is a refuge indeed.

4

The way of self is the way of sorrow ;
But Truth refreshes the weary, and lifts up the oppressed.
There is gladness for the grief-sticken,
And healing for them that are afflicted with the sorrows of the world.
There is a place of freedom where the chains of sin are broken,
Where weeping is not, and lamentation is no more heard.
There is a Friend for the friendless,
And consolation for them that have no comforter
Come; see; and receive.
Truth meets all needs, and is ready to receive all who come.
The righteous rest there ;
They have received the fulness of joy.
Let also the unrighteous come ;
Yea, let them that are weary of sin, come ;
And they that are burdened and oppressed with the sorrows of self,
Let them enter and be glad.
There is a Home for the homeless, and a Country for the exiled ;
For the wanderer there is a happy Way, and the lost have a City of Refuge.
Whosoever will turn, let him turn and come.
Truth brings joy out of sorrow, and peace out of perturbation;
It points the selfish to the Way of Good, and sinners to the Path of Holiness.
Its spirit is the doing of righteousness.
To the earnest and faithful it brings consolation ;
Upon the obedient and skilful it bestows the crown of peace.
I take refuge in Truth :
Yea, in the spirit of Good, in the knowledge of Good, and in the doing of Good I abide,
And I am reassured and comforted.

13

It is to me as though malice were not, and hatred had vanished away.
Lust is confined to the nethermost darkness,
It hath no way in Truth's transcendent Light.
Pride is broken up and dissolved.
And vanity is melted away as a mist.
I have set my face towards the Perfect Good, and my feet in the Blameless Way ;
And because of this I am consoled.
I am strengthened and comforted, having found refuge in Truth.

Truth as Redeemer

1

TRUTH is our Redeemer.
Truth purifies our hearts and bestows upon us the glorious gift of divine Love.
There is no salvation in selfishness.
Self is the vessel of sin and the receptacle of sorrow ;
But when we fly to Truth, self is ended, and Love abides for ever.
We have tried the ways of self, and we know how hard they are.
We also look upon the weary multitudes, and compassion is stirred within us :
But now we have found the Truth the pilgrimage of self is ended,
Our feet are rested, and there is no more weariness of heart.
The nature of self is error;
It cannot, therefore, comprehend Truth.
The experience of self is suffering;
It cannot, therefore, apprehend bliss.
When the vessel of self is broken, and its contents of error and suffering are scattered,
Then is Truth revealed and realised.
Truth alone can comprehend Truth, and bliss apprehendeth bliss.
How can self know Love, seeing that its nature is its own gratification ?
How can it know peace, seeing that it cannot bestow Love ?
How can it enter into salvation, seeing that it dreads the loss of its

14

perishable lusts and empty pleasures ?
Self is the way of darkness and the path of pain.
The redeemed have put away self, and have accepted Truth.
Self regards error as Truth, when it is pleasing;
It regards Truth as error, when it is displeasing;
Seeking pleasure and dreading pain, it does not know good and evil.
Truth knows Truth as Truth, and error as error;
It avoids evil and chooses good, without considerations of pleasure and pain.
Divine Love is the perfect flower of Truth;
For when Truth fills the heart Love blossoms out in the life.
By this flower is Truth known,
For wheresoever-impartial Love is, there is Truth.
Just deeds, pure actions, works untainted with self, minds controlled and calm,–
These are the angelic messengers of Truth ;
The possessors of these are the redeemed ;
Their habitation is peace.

2

Truth is the Saviour of the world.
There is no other Saviour.
There can be no compromise with Truth ;
It says "Give up self."
Truth is our Redeemer only when we yield up all to it.
Self cannot be saved.
It must be abandoned.
It must be left to the darkness in which it originated and to which it belongs.
The light of Salvation is only for them that press forward, and leave all selfishness behind.
And they who turn not back enter the presence of the Redeemer,
They are clothed with His Glory.
Who can see the glory of the redeemed ?
The redeemed behold it,
And them that are about to be redeemed, see it dimly:
But the eyes of the world are holden with the thought of self.

The redeemed are silent in the midst of men.
They accuse not, condemn not, revile not.
When smitten, they are not angry,
And when mocked, they make no sign.
Vet him that smote them they succour in his sorrow ;
And when they that mocked them are brought low,
They lift them up and bless them.
The utterance of Truth is deeds.
The redeemed are freed from all selfishness.
They are made perfect in Truth.
The thought of self being eliminated, there is nothing remaining in
them that can give rise to selfishness.
They are calm and just, doing that which is right, and passion is
purged from their actions.
He who comes to the feet of Truth,
Earnest in thought, strong in will, and contrite in heart,
Will be lifted up and saved.
He will overcome all that defiles, and all that causes sorrow.
The light of Truth will light up his mind, dispelling all darkness,
And he will stand among them to whom the Cosmic Glory is
unveiled.
For, to the redeemed, the narrow confiness of self are burst and
broken asunder,
And the mind is conscious of the Eternal.
The universe is known as it is;
Yea, its perfection and the splendour of its Law are revealed.
So large, so boundless, so all-embracing is the life of the redeemed
in Truth.

3

Immortal Truth redeems us from mortal error.
Clinging no more to the perishable, we fly to the Imperishable,
And find the Rock of Safety.
The body grows old, it withers and decays:
Passions burn out, leaving only the ashes of regret:
Pleasures cease to satisfy and pains fill up their places;
But Truth is imperishable;
It never grows old, nor does it wither and decay;

It does not consume, and it leaves behind no sorrow and no pain.
To set the mind upon that which is perishable;
To be consumed by violent passions;
To live in unhappiness and misery,–
This it is to be unredeemed.
The redeemed having the knowledge of the Imperishable and being
in possession of righteousness,
Live in happiness and joy,
For Truth is always bright and beautiful.
Yea, Truth is always peace - bestowing;
It calms the storms of strife ;
To the passion - driven it brings quiet;
Upon the dark waters of anguish it pours the oil of stillness ;
The mind that is troubled it restores, and envelops it with silence.
The redeemed are satisfied;
They are in security and peace ;
They are not overtaken by the storms of passion,
Nor attacked and laid low by fierce desires:
They abide in the Place of Safety.
What enemy shall overcome the redeemed !
Have they not slain the supreme enemy, even self!
Have they not taken his stronghold even their own hearts !
Yea, they have purified their hearts, and the impure cannot
overcome the pure.
Out of the black night !
Out of the fierce war ;
Out of the confusion and the conflict have the redeemed come;
And now they dwell in the Light ;
They abide with peace, and darkness and strife are no more.

4

The unredeemed are in the confines of self ;
They are surrounded with darkness;
They seek for self only.
The redeemed are in the glory of the universal, the impersonal ;
They are surrounded with light ;
They seek the good of all.
Truth is the breaker of bonds;

It liberates the slave ;
It sets the captive free.
Who chooses bondage rather than liberty ?
Who prefers darkness to light ?
He who has not known liberty loves his chains;
And he who has not seen the light prefers to remain in darkness.
And when liberty is made known it is desired.
When light is perceived, there is no longer a dwelling - place in
darkness.
The desires of the flesh are a tormenting fever;
The hatreds, conflicts, and covetings of the mind are a consuming
fire :
But there is a healing for the fever, and a water for the quenching
of the fire.
Truth is the healer of the mind ;
It is a sweet medicine to the afflicted,
And a draught of cool water to them that are troubled with thirst.
There is no unrest in Truth.
The unredeemed are in the way of sorrow ;
Pain and weariness are their companions.
Reaching after pleasures, they grasp sorrows ;
Striving eagerly for self, happiness departs from them.
But the redeemed are in the Way of Gladness;
Strength and joy are their companions ;
And not departing from Good they dwell in the House of
Happiness.
From what, then, are we redeemed ?
From what are we saved, and where is our salvation ?
We are redeemed from self and passion,
From sin and sorrow,
From unholiness and unrest,
Even from these are we taken away,
We are saved from lust and hatred,
From pride and vanity,
From covetousness and envy,
Even from these are we drawn away.
We are saved by the Truth ;
By the practice of Truth,
By the knowledge of Truth,

And by the power of Truth.
Our salvation is from the Truth.
In Truth we rest.
Truth is the Redeemer of the world.

Truth as Reconciler

1

TRUTH is the Reconciler of Extremes.
It neutralises all opposites.
It harmonises all discords and contradictions.
It brings back to us harmony and peace.
When we were in error we saw all things as erroneous.
Yea, when we were blind to our own error we saw error in all else;
We saw good as evil, and evil as good ;
Light as darkness, and darkness as light;
But now we have plucked out the eye of error from ourselves, we
see the Supreme Good.
Truth reconciles man to man;
It reconciles man to the universe ;
It bestows upon him the knowledge of the Good Law;
It reveals the hidden justice in all events.
In error is unrest, and anger, and perturbation.
Trouble and turmoil is ever with him, who sees injustice,
confusion, and contradiction;
But he who sees Justice, Order, and Harmony is calm and filled
with peace.
Error sees error; and Truth sees Truth.
Error, being darkness, cannot penetrate the light;
But Truth, being light, can penetrate the darkness.
Truth reconciles darkness with light.
Error is the Great Unrest ;
Truth is the Great Peace.
He who looks with the eye of error is restless as the shifting winds.
But restful as the stable mountain is he who looks with the eye of
Truth.
We are reconciled to the world;

We are reconciled to humanity;
And being thus reconciled we are at rest.
Where unrest is, there is no reconciliation ;
And they who are not so reconciled have not received the Truth.

2

All things are proportionate ;
All circumstances are just;
All events are of causation.
He who has received the Light of Truth sees all things in their right relations.
All things are ruled by causation;
All things are of the nature of causation;
There is nothing which is not contained in cause and effect.
Cause and effect are one :
The Divine Law is one
Out of chaos into Cosmos have we come;
Out of confusion into harmony;
Out of bewilderment into peace perpetual.
There is good in all things.
Out of evil comes suffering;
Out of suffering comes sorrow;
And from sorrow is lowly wisdom born.
Though the night be long, the Morning comes;
And with it comes sunshine and singing.
Though the world be in its long night, the Great Day will dawn.
Lo ! we behold the splendour of its Light !
There are no more any enemies ;
All are our own, our beloved;
Both them that bless and them that curse all are friendly to us.
The inward enemy being overcome, all outward foes have vanished away.
There is no more enmity.
Men and things are in their right places.
There is no more strife;
No more fighting ;
No more warfare.
We behold the fray, but do not engage in it ;

We hear the tumult, and we make no sound.
But though quiescent, we watch;
Though silent, we are not indifferent.
Perceiving the Divine Order, we are reconciled to all things;
And being so reconciled, we are in perfect peace.

3

Wherefore should we mourn and be sorrowful?
The very ground of lamentation is dissolved;
The foundation of sorrow is cut away ;
And as for sin and evil–they were, but are not.
The sphere of controversy is broken :
About what should we contend?
The world of division is annulled :
What have we to defend?
Can Truth fail, that we should argue, that we should be anxious
and concerned ?
Because Truth endures for ever, our peace can never fail.
The seed fails in its appointed place;
The flower appears, and also the fruit in its season;
Day warms, and night cools; Light is shed, and rain falls;
Snow covers, and frost binds.–
Are these things opposed ?
Are they enemies?
They work together as one.
Who, then, shall stir us up to wrath?
Who shall draw us into the lists of contention?
With them that agree with us we are at peace?
And with that oppose us we are also at peace.
Friends are not near, nor enemies far ;
Praise and blame are not asunder.
Truth draws all things together;
It resolves all opposites into one.
Yea, forces that seemed divided are now united ;
Things that seemed to contend are now in agreement;
And events that seemed adverse are now friendly.
How foolish we were in our fear !
How blind in our bigotry !

How hateful in our heart !
We were as the beasts that rage and kill,
Or as the blind beetle that dashes on to its death !
All things are in unison ;
And fear, and blindness, and hatred are no more.
Having departed from the lesser, the Greater is revealed :
Having renounced the part, the Whole is received :
Having abandoned the imperfect, what remains but the Perfect !

4

Truly all things are reconciled, and peace awaits.
The Door of Truth is open.
None hinders, but man holds back.
He holds back for a time, and in the hour of ripeness he comesforward.
Whosoever will come, let him come ! Let him enter and be glad.
All things are now.
All Light, all Law, all Truth is now.
Time and Eternity are one ;
Matter and Spirit are one;
Death and Life are one;
The blind see not,
But they that have eyes know the things which they see.
We strive not;
We stand apart and are silent.
Men hurry to and fro a little while ;
A little time they come, and a little time they go :
How eager they are I How anxious !
How fierce !
Better than all worldly gain is the spirit of peace.
Better than rule and riches is the Reconciliation of Truth.
Fires burn out, and storms subside ;
But serenity remains.
Calmness preserves and restores, and Tranquillity is a great possession.
Who condemns our aloofness?
Him our peace enfolds ;
Even him our reconciliation embraces.

Apart, we are not separate :
Aloof, we are not estranged :
Engaging with none, and joining with none, Yet we belong to all.
For the Perfect Reconciliation is not partial, but just.
He who sees all sides, sees the Whole ;
And seeing the Whole, he is satisfied;
Being satisfied, he is peace with all. Seers of the great Glory;
Hearers of the Heavenly Harmony;
Knowers of the Perfect Law—
Great is your gladness !
Wondrous is your wisdom !
Deep is your peace !
More powerful is one day of your silence than a thousand years of noise.
All parties, all sides, all religions are reconciled.
Love supports all, sustains all, nourishes ad.
The Great Reconciler is come ;
He is here, and we have found Him.
We sought Him, and He turned not away ;
And because of this, we have received the world;
And peace does not depart from us.

Truth as Protector

GOOD deeds are Truth.
Our good deeds remain with us, they save and protect us.
Evil deeds are error.
Our evil deeds follow us, they overthrow us in the hour of temptation.
The evil-doer is not protected from sorrow ;
But the good-doer is shielded from all harm.
The fool says unto his evil deed—
"Remain thou hidden, be thou unexposed,"
But his evil is already published, and his sorrow is sure.
If we are in evil, what shall protect us ?
What keep us from misery and confusion ?
Nor man nor woman, nor wealth nor power, nor heaven nor earth shall keep us from confusion.

From the results of evil there is no escape ;
No refuge and no protection.
If we are in Good, what shall overthrow us ?
What bring us to misery and confusion?
Nor man nor woman, nor poverty nor sickness, nor heaven nor
earth shall bring us to confusion.
The effects of Good appear, though the cause be forgotten,
And its refuge and protection is at hand.
What can amulets and charms avail ?
What can the muttering of set prayers avail ?
What can the observance of formal rites avail ?
They cannot avail, they are empty;
They are without efficacy, and are void of protection.
Righteousness avails.
The doing of good deeds avails.
A pure heart and a blameless life avail.
They are filled with joy and peace.
Truth is a happy retreat and an eternal protection.
In Truth there is no more doubt and uncertainty.
There is safety and security :
There is a straight way and a quiet rest.

2

The righteous know the protection of Truth.
Their minds are free, and they are happy-hearted.
Empty excuses and vain quibbles they harbour not.
They scheme not how to protect themselves ;
Their deeds are invincible defenders;
Their lives bear witness, and they are not ashamed.
The unrighteous are overtaken with shame and confusion.
They try to hide, but cannot ;
They have no place of concealment:
Their deeds accuse them, and they have no protection.
How happy are the righteous!
They are relieved from all anxiety.
Walking with Truth, they walk in perfect freedom.
How fearless are the righteous !
They have no dark forebodings ;

They dread no evil;
When evil threatens they are calm and unafraid.
Truth shields from the afflictions of the mind.
It fortifies against misery ;
It destroys self - delusion and sorrow.
The Light of Truth reveals error and the cause of error;
It also reveals the effects of error ;
It frees the mind from all subjection to evil.
He that is established in Truth is established in safety.
Truth cannot proceed from error, nor error from Truth.
Good cannot be the effect of evil, nor evil the effect of Good.
This is little understood.
But the righteous understand, and, understanding, they are glad ;
They rejoice in the Law of Truth.
The understanding mind is not misled by appearances:
It rejoices in Good against all appearances.
When events press, it does not think, "The Good has failed ";
When outward things fail, it does not say, "Righteousness has not supported me ";
When persecution comes, it cannot say, "Lo! Truth affords me no protection !"
Truth is in the thought, and not in the thing ;
It resides in the hearts, and not in the outward habit ;
It destroys the inward enemies, and the outward reverses have no more pover;
Their sting is gone, their evil is dispersed.
The peace of the perfect ones can never be destroyed.

3

The pure in heart are protected from within.
The perfect indeed are guarded by Good :
They are upheld by the Good Law.
By the knowledge of Truth they are lifted up:
They stand and do not fall.
Truth cannot be overtaken by error ;
It cannot be overturned by man.
Error passes away but the Truth remains.
Men fall, but the Truth remains.

Truth cannot change ;
It is eternal and indestructible.
Herein is the salvation of the wise ;
Herein is the protection of the pure ;
Herein is the joy of the perfect—
That, being one with Truth, they have come to peace eternal.
He who is one with Truth, reflects Truth.
He is steadfast, fearless, serene.
He changes not, but is always true.
When tried, he does not falter ;
When assailed, he does not fall.
Permanent in purity and peace, he is established in gentleness and strength.
Who mourns for sin ?
Who gropes for deliverance?
Who searches for the permanent ?
Let him make himself pure :
Let him come to Truth ;
Let him find peace in the practice of Good.
Things are impermanent;
They have no abiding protection.
Truth is permanent;
Its protection abides through all changes.
Ill deeds are exposed in torment and confusion;
Good deeds are established in bliss and wisdom.
Truth is a Friend that does not disappoint ;
A Protector that never fails.
The world fails ;
It fades and passes like a dream Truth stands;
It becomes more distinct and real.
They who have found Truth are satisfied.
Protected by Truth, they have found a
Protector indeed.
The patient are protected from impatience.
The pure are protected from impurity.
The humble are protected from pride.
The loving are protected from hatred.
Greed flees from the presence of the open-handed ;
Into the habitations of the peaceful strife cannot come ;

And folly walks not where tread the footsteps of the wise.
Truth is its own security ;
It protects without premeditation.
It dispenses with disguises, and shields by its own inherent reality.
Its light disposes of all darkness ;
It exposes the false and reveals the true.
Error falls before Truth ;
Its shield is shattered, its sword broken ;
Yea, it is laid low, and cannot rise.
It is helpless and has nor champion nor defender.
Truth does not fall before error.
The powerless cannot overcome the powerful.
The lesser cannot subdue the greater.
The slave does not command the master.
All things are subject to Truth.
Truth is a shield to the righteous ;
A shelter to the pure ;
A light upon the pathway of the just.
Truth is supreme ;
Truth is invincible ;
Truth is triumphant for ever and ever.

Part II: The Divine Dialogue

I, the Master,
Dwell in the hearts of all men, but all men do not consciously dwell with me:
He that abides with me in all his thoughts and deeds, has reached the Divine Consummation.

The Divine Dialogue between the Master and the Disciple

Salutation

REJOICE, all ye who seek Truth !
Be glad and not sorrowful, all ye who love Truth!
For your sorrows shall pass away as the mists of the morning ;

Your doubts shall be as the darkness that is not;
And as a dream of the night shall your afflictions be.
The disciple cried, and lo ! the Master heard;
The disciple was ready, and lo ! the Master was at hand;
The disciple sought, and behold ! the Master revealed.

1. Of Seeking and Finding

Disciple. Where is knowledge ?
Where is Truth ?
Where is peace ?
I am sorrowful, and find no comfort in men;
I have gone astray, and find no surety in the teachings of men ;
Yea, even in myself I find no Truth, and no remedy for my doubt
and sorrow
I have striven in the pride of my heart :
I have contended with men for my opinions ;
I have mistaken evil for good, and have called ignorance
knowledge ;
And now I am alone, and there is none to hear me,
And if I cry, there is none to hear my voice.
Master. Nay, I am with thee, and I hear thy voice.
Disciple. Who art thou that dost assure, me ?
Master. I am the Spirit of Truth.
Disciple. O Master ! O Spirit of Truth !
Why didst thou not come to me before ?
Why didst thou leave me so long desolate ?
Master. Thou wert not desolate till now;
Pride was thy companion, and pride satisfied thee.
Where pride is, there I cannot come,
And he who listens to its flatteries, cannot hear my Voice.
Self - glory blinded thee, so that my Form thou couldst not see :
Self - exultation deafened thee, and when I called, thou didst not
hear;
Self - seeking led thee astray, and my Way was hidden from thee.
But now, having put away pride, thou hast both seen and heard.
Ask, and I will answer ;
Seek, and thou shalt find.

Disciple. Comfort me, O Master! for I am weary ;
Strengthen me, for I am weak ;
Teach me, for I am lacking in knowledge.
Master. He who deserts self, and takes refuge in me, is never deserted ;
My Word is his comfort,
My Law his strength,
And my commands his Instruction and Knowledge.
Disciple. Speak thy Word, and I will listen;
Reveal thy Law, and I will walk therein ;
Command me, and I, thy servant, will obey ;
For thou art the Master whom I so long sought,
And having found thee, let me not depart from thee.
Master. He who follows self, abandons me;
But he who abandons self, lo ! he is with me always.
Disciple. Hitherto I have clung to self ;
I have followed after vain and empty desires ;
And caught in the toils of self - delusion, I have not known thy presence;
But now, O Master! I have found thee ;
And having found thee, let me remain with thee;
Let me be thy child, obeying thy voice ;
Let me be thy pupil, receiving thy instruction;
Let me become thy disciple, and fo low wheresoever thou dost lead.
Master. Thy humility, O disciple ! hath made the mine.
Thou hast entered the Gateway leading to my Kingdom,
Even to the Kingdom of a righteous life.
Henceforth thou wilt follow Truth and not self;
Striving, thou hast entered ;
Searching, thou hast revealed ;
Seeking, thou hast found.
Ask whatsoever thou wilt and I will not withhold instruction.

2. Of Entering the Way

Disciple. Teacher of teachers, instruct thou me.
Master. Ask, and I will answer.

Disciple. I have read much, but am ignorant still ;
I have studied the doctrines of the schools, but have not become wise thereby ;
I know the Scriptures by heart, but peace is hidden from me.
Point out to me, O Master! the way of knowledge,
Reveal to me the high way of divine wisdom,
Lead thou thy child into the path of peace.
Master. The way of knowledge, O disciple, is by searching the heart;
The highway of wisdom is by the practice of righteousness ;
And by a sinless life is found the way of peace.
Disciple. Bear with me, O Master ! in my uncertainty.
I am bewildered by the multitude of opinions,
And by the number of schools am I confounded;
Delusion blinds me, doubt encompasses me,
And I cannot find the way wherein I should walk.
Teach me how to search,
How to practise,
How to wear the garment of a blameless life.
Master. Delusion and doubt, O disciple ! are within thyself;
Within thyself, also, are reality and certainty.
By thine own errors only art thou blinded,
Remove those errors, and thou shalt behold Truth.
Engage, therefore, in holy meditation ;
Search thy heart with the searching of Truth,
And cast out therefrom all that is of self.
Disciple. What is of self ?
Master. Desire and passion and egotism.
From desire and passion and egotism springs self - delusion ;
And self-delusion is the obscuration of Truth.
Renounce desire ;
Overcome passion ;
Put away egotism,
Then will delusion be dispelled, and all thy doubts will vanish.
Disciple. O Master ! great is the task which thou hast set before me,
Laborious the work which thou commandest me to do,
Steep and strange the way of renunciation which thou hast pointed out to me.

Desire is deeply rooted in my nature,
And passion binds me fast to earthly things,
Yea, desire and passion are my very self ;
Must I renounce myself ?
Must I yield up that which seems so sweet ?
All men long to preserve the self ;
They pray for its eternal preservation and possession,
And must I let it perish ?
Master. Thou must, for thou hast vowed to follow me.
Disciple. Yea, I have vowed, and I will follow thee.
Master. Seest thou how all men suffer ?
This is because they long to preserve the self;
This is because they labour for its eternal preservation and possession.
In desire and egotism and passion are turmoil and unrest,
In me alone is peace ;
Weary and pain - stricken is the world because it knows not me ;
But in me there is no weariness,
And pain and sorrow cannot come to my abode.
My abode is a purified heart ;
The upright mind is my temple ;
And the blameless life is my holy habitation.
Disciple. I will take refuge in thee ;
In thy abode ;
In thy temple ;
Yea, even in thy holy habitation.
Master. The purified heart is not stained by desire ;
The upright mind is not impelled by passion ;
And in the blameless life there is no thought of self.
Search thy heart, and follow Truth ;
Put away the self of desire and passion and egotism,
Deny, overcome, and abandon it ;
Let no vestige of it remain with thee,
For it is the author of all confusion,
The source of all affliction,
The spring of pain and sorrow and unrest.
Rest thou in me.
Disciple. Thou hast pointed out to me the way of Truth,
Even the holy way of selfishness.

31

That way will I walk ;
My resolution, O Master of Truth ! is fixed in thee.
I will put away desire, and will cling to thee ;
I will be deaf to the voices of passion, and will listen only to thy voice ;
I will not seek my own, but will obey the holy Law.
Lo ! I have put my feet upon thy way.
Lead thou thy servant unto light and peace.
Master. Thou hast entered, O disciple ! the path of righteousness;
Thy feet are set upon the way of wisdom ;
Thou shalt comprehend my Law,
The light of knowledge shall illumine thee.
And I will guide thy footfalls unto peace.

3. Of Discipline and Purification

Disciple. I am in sorrow, O Master!
My feet are weary, and darkness is closing around me ;
Desert me not, but come now to my assistance !
My desires are strong, and they cry out for their habitual pleasures ;
My passions are violent, and overwhelm me with their strength ;
And the voices of my false opinions weary me with their demands.
The way is dark and difficult to follow ;
Shed upon me, O Master ! the light of thy knowledge,
Comfort me with the balm of thy instruction.
Master. Thy sorrow, O disciple ! is of the self ;
In me there is no sorrow.
The darkness which surrounds thee is the shadow cast by the self ;
There is no darkness in me.
Truth is serene and sorrowless ;
There is no weeping and weariness and lamentation in Truth.
Even now, though thou seest it not, my light is shining on thy pathway ;
But thou seest only the dark illusions of thy worldly self ;
Press forward, and think only of Truth ;
Look not behind thee, nor let thy mind swerve from thy holy resolution ;

Great is the conquest Which thou hast entered
upon, Even the mighty conquest of thy self;
Be faithful, and thou shalt overcome.
Disciple. Lead me, O Master ! for my darkness is very great ;
Clouds of selfish thoughts envelop me,
And the enemies within my mind assail me continually ;
In the snares of my own making my feet are caught,
And when I think to walk firmly I stumble and fall ;
Yea, my falls are many and grievous, and my wounds frequent and
sore.
Will the darkness lift, O Master ?
Will trial end in victory ?
And will there be an end to my many sorrows?
Master. When thy heart is pure, the darkness will disappear ;
When thy mind is freed from passion, thou wilt reach the end of
trial,
And when the thought of self - preservation is yielded up, there
will be no more cause for sorrow.
Thou art now upon the way of discipline and purification ;
All my disciples must walk that way.
Before thou canst enter the white light of Knowledge,
Before thou canst behold the full glory of Truth,
All thy impurities must be purged away,
The delusions dispelled,
And thy mind fortified with endurance.
Though darkness surroundeth thee,
Though temptation assaileth thee on every hand,
Though thou art sore distressed, and seest not before thee,
Yet relax not thy faith in Truth ;
Forget not that Truth is eternally supreme,
Remember that I, the Lord of Truth, am watching over thee.
Disciple. Great is my faith in Truth ;
And I will not forget, but will remember thee.
Master. Walking faithfully the path of discipline and purification,
Not forsaking and abandoning it,
And not longing to enjoy the pleasures which thou hast left behind
thee,
Thou wilt learn those things which are necessary for thee ;
Thou wilt learn of the nature of sin and the meaning of temptation ;

Of suffering and sorrow, and their cause and cure;
Of the fleeting nature of thy self, and its pleasures ;
Of the permanence of Truth and its abiding peace ;
Of what are the marks of ignorance, and what constitutes
knowledge ;
Of what makes evil and what is eternally good;
Of the painfullness of self and the bliss of Truth wilt thou learn,
Thou wilt also learn of illusion and Reality.
Be faithful and endure, and I will teach thee all things.
Disciple. I will not turn my face from thee,
Nor will I desert thy holy Way.
Master. Hear me again, O disciple !
Walking faithfully the path of discipline and purification,
Not abandoning it, but submitting to its austerities,
Thou wilt acquire the three lesser powers of discipleship;
Thou wilt also receive the three greater powers ;
And the lesser and the greater powers will render the invincible ;
By their aid thou wilt subdue all sin ;
Thou wilt overcome to the uttermost ;
Thou wilt achieve the Supreme Conquest.
Disciple. What are the lesser and the greater powers ?
Master. Self - control, self - reliance, and watchfulness–
These are the three lesser powers.
Steadfastness, Patience, and Gentleness–
These are the three greater powers.
When thy mind is well controlled, and in thy keeping,
When thou reliest upon no external help, but upon Truth alone,
And when thou art ceaselessly watchful over thy thoughts and
actions–
Then will the three lesser powers be thine,
And with these powers thou wilt dispel the Great Darkness,
Thou wilt approach the Supreme Light ;
Approaching the Supreme Light, thou wilt become steadfastly
fixed in Truth.
Thou wilt become patient with an infinite patience,
And gentle with a gentleness which nothing can change or mar ;
Then will the three greater powers be thine ;
Then wilt thou come to the end of the path of discipline,
And wilt ascend unto the higher path of knowledge ;

Walking the path of knowledge thy sorrow will cease.
Thy darkness will pass away for ever,
And joy and light will wait upon thy footsteps.
Disciple. I am reassured, O Master ! and am strong to proceed :
I am obedient to thee, and will submit to thy discipline,
For thou hast comforted me with the word of knowledge ;
Thou hast strengthened me with the exhortation of Truth.
Thou hast instructed me with the instruction of enlightenment.
Master. Blessed is he who obeys the Truth,
He shall not remain comfortless, but shall receive the benediction
of peace.

4. Of Renunciation

Disciple. Teacher divine ! Thy light is breaking in upon my mind,
I now know the cause of my sorrow and suffering ;
I apprehend the sorrows of mankind,
For my sufferings are the sufferings of the world ;
I see that sorrow and suffering are rooted in self.
That evil and woe are in the desires of self,
And that all the desires of self must be relin-guished,
Guide me, O Master ! into the way of self-sacrifice ;
Teach me how to abolish self from the mind;
Reveal to me the truth about renunciation.
Master. Renunciation, O disciple ! is twofold;
There is renunciation in the letter ;
There is also renunciation in the spirit.
The renunciation of outward things and particular acts only—
This is the false renunciation in the letter ;
The renunciation of inward desires and defilements—
This is the true renunciation in the spirit.
Beware, O learner ! of the renunciation which is false ;
Perform thou the renunciation which is true.
Disciple. Instruct me further in the renunciation which is according
to Truth,
Then I will embrace and perform it;
So shall I avoid the renunciation which is erroneous and

misleading.

Master. Seek no gratification in the things which thou doest ;
Look not for reward in the things wherein thou strivest ;
Do all thy duties meekly, putting away desire—
This is the true renunciation.
Do not think of gain or loss to thyself ,—
Think not to obtain pleasure and avoid pain in thy acts ;
Do all things faithfully that are necessary to be done—
This also is the true renunciation.
Sever not thyself from the world,
But relingnish all love for the world and its pleasures ;
Do thy work in the world without thought of personal ends—
This, again, is the true renunciation.
Not by the outer things of the world is a man defiled ;
He is defiled by the low desires of his heart.
To renounce the world, and not to relinguish to clinging to self—
This is the false renunciation.
Not from riches or poverty,
Not from wife or children,
Not from power and servitude—
Not from these things do afflictions spring.
From indolence and self - indulgence,
From lust and coveteousness,
From hatred and pride—
From these things only do afflictions spring.
Renounce the evil within, and the things of the world will not
defile thee ;
Put away all thought of self, and whatsoever thou doest it will
bring to thee no suffering;
In all thy duties forsake the thought of self, and sorrow will never
overtake thee.
He who quitteth a duty that is irksome,
Seeking happiness thereby ;
He who fleeth from the scene of temptation.
Seeking strength thereby;
He who abandoneth his obligations,
Seeking bliss thereby,—
Such a man, O disciple ! falsely renounces ;
He is deluded, and will not attain to purity of heart.

As a brave soldier, when death is inevitable does not desert his
post,
Thinking of duty only, and not of self-preservation,
So he who renounces truely, remains in his place in the world,
Performing all his duties steadfastly, not thinking of self.
Renounce self, O disciple !
Renounce all the tendencies of self;
Renounce all the passions and prejudices of self;
Renounce all the errors and egotism of self;
Such is the true renunciation ;
Such is the sacrifice which leads to enlightenment and peace.
Disciple. What, O Master! are the tendencies of the self ?
Master. Lust and self-indulgence,
Self - seeking and avarice,
Hatred and anger,
Vanity and pride,
Doubt and fear–
These are the tendencies of self;
These are the things that must be renounced
; *Disciple.* And these things, O spirit immaculate ! I will renounce ;
I will obliterate them from my mind ;
I will abolish them from my inmost heart ;
For now I see how they lead men into ways of blindless ;
That they make snares of suffering for the feet of men ;
That they dig deep pits of sorrow for men to fall therein.
I rejoice, O Divine One ! in that which thou hast revealed to me ;
For thou hast opened unto me the highway of holiness ;
Thou hast pointed out to me the straight path
of peace;
Thou hast shown me how to walk the sure way of wisdom.
Thee will I follow; lead me to thy Law.
Master. Blessed is he who follows where I lead ;
He shall ascend unto high and Heavenly Places;
He shall behold with the vision that is faultless ;
He shall see with the eye of truth which comprehendeth all things.

5. Of Purity of Heart

Disciple. While I am undergoing thy discipline and purification,
While walking the holy way of renunciation,
Let me behold the beauty of thy Purity ;
Reveal to me the Purity which is divine ;
For I would know the Highest, even Truth :
I would gaze upon thy face, O Master !
I would behold thy glory ;
I would see thee as thou art.
Master. He who rightly renounces,
Who humbly purges his heart of self,
Who diligently searches for Truth not for selfish pleasures,
He, my lonely one, shall find my Purity ;
He, my faithful one, shall surely see my face,
He, my chosen one, shall come to me at last.
Disciple. Thou art my refuge and my dwelling-place ;
My eyes, I know, will rest on thee at last ;
My heart at last will stay itself on thee.
Show me the highest and holiest way,
Even the stainless way of Purity.
Master. Thou art ready to be washed free from thy defilements ;
As a vessel thou art ready to be cleansed ;
And when thou art cleansed thou shalt be filled with the pure
Water of Truth.
By these four things is the heart defiled—
The craving for pleasures,
The clinging to temporal things,
The love of self,
The lust for personal continuance:
From these four defilements spring all sins and sorrows Wash thou
thy heart ;
Put away sensual cravings ;
Detach the mind from the wish for possession;
Abandon self defence and self-importance ;
And do not long for personal immortality.
Thus putting away all cravings, thou wilt attain to satisfaction;
Detaching thy mind from the love of perishable things, thou wilt
acquire wisdom;
Abandoning the thought of self, thou wilt come to peace ;
And not lusting for eternal life, thou wilt realise the incorruptible

Truth.

He is pure who is free from desire ;
Who does not crave for sensual excitements ;
Who sets no value on perishable things;
Who is the same in riches and poverty,
In success or failure,
In victory or defeat,
In life or death;
Who does not set up his own opinions ;
Who is willing not to be ;
Lo ! he it is who possesses my Pureness ;
His happiness remains;
His rest is sure ;
His peace is not disturbed;
He knows what constitutes holiness ;
He understands the stainlessness of Truth.
Disciple. I will cleanse my heart with the cleansing of Truth ;
I will be pure as thou art pure ;
I will put away the thought of pleasure ;
I will not covet perishable things;
My personality I will regard as of no importance,
Ceasing to crave for its eternal continuance.
Death comes to all men, and the tears of sorrow flow ;
But Truth is eternal, and its knowledge leads to peace.
I followed self, but it was filled with pain;
I followed the world but it was fraught with heavy sorrow ;
But now, O Master of Truth I follow thee,
And thou art leading me to bliss unspeakable ;
Thou directest my steps into the way of purity and peace.
Master. Be strenuous in effort,
Strong in resolution ;
Patient in endurance;
So wilt thou overcome all sin;
Thou wilt become divinely pure;
Sorrow and pain thou wilt altogether subdue
And thou wilt acquire joy and strength and equanimity.

6. Of Righteousness

Master. Stand up, Son of Light I and put on the garment of
righteousness ;
Rejoice ! and enter the glad way of holiness ;
Open thine eyes, and behold the glory of Truth;
For thou hast been faithful and obedient;
Thou hast been patient and enduring ;
Thou hast conquered and overcome.
The Great Enemy, even self, thou hast slain;
The Great Darkness, even the darkness of ignorance, thou hast
dispersed ;
The Great Veil, even the veil of illusion, thou hast torn asunder.
Henceforth thou shalt walk in the way of knowledge,
Thou shalt dwell with peace,
Thou shalt bask in the light of immortality.
Rise up, Son of Truth ! in my divine dignity;
Put on the shining life of righteousness;
For thou art no longer self, thou art Truth,
Thy deeds will be according to the Eternal,
And thou wilt be a beacon to mankind.
Disciple. Now, O Master ! I see thee as thou art;
I see thy ineffable beauty and glory.
How can darkness dwell where thou art ?
How can sin and sorrow approach thee ?
I am dazzled by the power of thy majesty ;
Thou art Truth ! Thou art the Eternal!
And he who knoweth thee, liveth in thy light;
He doeth the deeds of light and not of darkness.
Point out to me now, O Master ! the righteous way ;
Reveal unto me the jewels of the perfect life ;
Instruct me in the doing which is according to the Eternal,
So that I may be watchful, and fail not.
Master. Unrighteous is he whose acts are born of self;
Righteous is he whose acts are born of Truth:
The unrighteous man is swayed by his feelings ;
Likes and dislikes are his masters ;
Prejudices and partialities blind him ;
Desiring and suffering,
Craving and sorrowing,
Self - control he knows not, and great is his unrest.

The righteous man is master of his moods ;
Likes and dislikes he has abandoned as childish things;
Prejudice and partiality he has put away.
Desiring nothing, he does not suffer;
Not craving enjoyment, sorrow does not overtake him ;
Perfect in self-control, great peace abides with him;
Do not condemn, resent or retaliate;
Do not argue, or become a partisan ;
Maintain thy calmness with all sides;
Be just, and speak truth.
Act in gentleness, compassion, and charity;
Be infinitely patient:
Hold fast to Love, and let it shape thy doing :
Have goodwill to all, without distinction :
Think equally of all, and be disturbed by none;
Be thoughtful and wise, strong and kind-hearted.
Be watchful, that no thought of self again creep in and stain thee.
Think of thyself as abolished, dispersed :
In all thy doing think of the good of others and of the world,
And not of pleasure or reward to thyself.
Thou art no longer separate and divided from men,
Thou art one with all ;
No longer strive against others for thyself,
But sympathise with all;
Regard no man as thine enemy,
Thou art the friend of all men.
Be at peace with all;
Pour out compassion on all living things;
Let boundless charity adorn thy words and deeds–
Such is the glad way of Truth.
Such is the doing which is according to the Eternal.
Filled with joy is the right-doer,
He acts from principles which do not change and pass away ;
Abandoning personality, he has become a power ;
He is one with the Eternal, and has passed beyond unrest.
The peace of the righteous man is perfect;
It is not disturbed by change and impermanence ;
Freed from passion, it is equal-minded, calm, and does not sorrow ;
He sees things as they are, and is no more confused.

Disciple. Thou has clothed me, O Master ! with righteousness ;
The perfect life thou hast revealed to me ;
Thou hast shown me the holy and the happy way.
Self is abolished, and I am thine ;
My thoughts are thy thoughts,
My words are thy words,
My deeds are thy deeds ;
Thou art eternal, and all my doing shall be from thee.
Allayed is the fever of life ;
Dispersed is all the darkness of the mind;
Uncertainty and unrest have vanished away;
Sin and suffering are ended, and peace abides for ever.
Master. Thou hast opened thine eyes to the Eternal Light;
Thou art no more self-deceived nor self-afflicted.
Enter now, O disciple ! the highway of divine knowledge,
And receive the bliss of immortality.

7. Of Knowledge of the Law

Disciple. Show unto me now, O Master ! the Perfect Knowledge ;
Reveal unto me the working of thy Law ;
Illuminate my mind with the wisdom of enlightenment,
Master. The Law of Life is perfect;
Nothing can be added to it or taken from it;
It cannot be altered or improved ;
None can avoid or escape it ;
Its operations are just;
It is eternal, and abides in the midst of change;
By it all things are protected, and there is no confusion :
The good is preserved in bliss and peace,
The evil is purified with punishment and suffering;
Knowledge it crowns with calmness,
Ignorance it scourges with unrest;
It works with twofold action :
It is Eternal Causation ;
It takes note of every thought and deed.
Thou hast attained, O disciple, to spiritual vision ;
Look now upon the world and tell me what thou seest.

Disciple. I see, O Master! the Great Darkness called Ignorance;
I see lurking therein the smouldering sparks of desire;
I see how those sparks gather strength;
They intensify into flaming passions ;
And over all mankind are heavy clouds of sorrow,
And these are for the quenching of passions.
Master. Thou hast well seen.
Look again, and say what thou beholdest.
Disciple. My sight hath pierced the cloudy veil of sorrow,
And above all I see the Great Light called Truth,
And there is no darkness therein,
No desires can enter there.
And there are no consuming passions ;
There is no weeping and no unrest.
Master. Thou hast seen, O disciple, the Law of Life ;
Thou hast perceived the twofold action of the Law.
There is ignorance which fosters desire ;
Desire is the painful hunger to obtain;
It is also the feverish clinging to that which is obtained;
Thence arises separation from the thing desired,
And this is suffering and sorrow.
From desire also arises egotism or selfishness,
Thus is created an illusory self,
And in the delusion of the self is the nightmare of the world's woe.
Thus man suffers by the action of the Law;
He can also escape suffering by the action of the Law.
When desire is abandoned, the painful hunger of the mind is cured,
The burning fever of clinging to things is assuaged,
And there is no separation and sorrow :
Thence arises union with all that is,
And this is satisfaction, bliss, and peace.
From non-desire also proceed Humility and Love;
The delusion of a permanent and separate individuality is destroyed ;
The preservation of the self is abandoned.
And thus is cut away the ground of hatred, and pride, and selfishness ;
Then arises holiness ;
The reality of things is revealed;

Truth is perceived, comprehended and known,
And this is the knowledge of the Law ;
This is the bliss of immortality.
Disciple. Very simple is the Law, O Truth ! yet who shall
comprehend it ?
Beautiful to behold, yet who can gaze upon it ?
Faultless in equity, yet who will listen, and receive it ?
Master. The pure-hearted one receives, beholds, and comprehends;
He acts with the action that is not attained by sin ;
His charity is without limit, it embraces all living things;
He perceives with the vision that does not err.
He does not condemn, knowing the Perfect Law,
And knowing the Perfect Law, he has entered into peace,
Disciple. Where knowledge is perfected, peace abides.
Great is the calmness of the wise.
Deep is the peace of the pure,
Perfect the bliss of them that know the Truth.
Stilled are the tempests of the mind,
There is no more perturbation.
There is a haven for the storm-tossed.
A home for them that are lost and forsaken.
A refuge for all who wander in the Night.
I have found thee, thou eternal One, at last !
Master. Thou hast sought and found ;
Thou hast fought and conquered ;
Thou hast striven and attained ;
He who has afflicted has become the healer of men :
The child has become the Instructor.
The pupil has become the Teacher.
The disciple and the Master are one;
What I am, that thou art.
Abide with Me in Peace.

Benediction

And now peace abides.
Self is dispersed and there is no more anguish;
Truth is attained, and affliction has ceased to be ;

44

The pilgrimage of pain is finished,
There is no more toil and darkness,
There is no more doubt and weeping,
Unrest and sorrow have vanished away.
Love folds the world; to all that suffer, Peace !

Part III: The Divine Messages

I, a Sower,
Cast forth this seed upon the broad plains of the world.
And leave it to the watchful care of the Supreme.

The Divine Messages

The First Prophecy, called the Awakening

SONS of Light, I salute you.
Children of the Morning, I greet you.
Awake ! arise! and rouse ye them that slumber!
I proclaim to you the advent of the Morning;
The dawn of the New Day is upon every living thing,
And down the holy Mountain cometh the Light of Love, the Lowly One,
Bringing good tidings and publishing peace.
And this is the majesty of the Morning,–
That evil shall flee from the valleys,
And hardly shall darkness find a lodging-place:
For where light is, there is no darkness ;
Where good is, evil is dispersed,
Where peace is, strife is destroyed;
Where love is, all hatred has ceased;
Where purity is, all sin is overcome,
And from the abode of Truth all error has fled away.
And this is the joy of the Morning,–
That evil is conquered, and Good is triumphant;
That the glory of Truth is revealed;
That the Path of Perfection is opened up,

And the bliss of a holy life is partaken of.
And this is the consummation of the
Morning,–
That darkness is dispelled by Light
Ignorance by Knowledge,
Illusion by Reality,
And error by Truth.
And the majesty of the Morning is revealed;
And the joy of the Morning is comprehended ;
And the consummation of the Morning is realised.
Ye who have waited, come now, and gaze your fill:
Upon the Heights the coming of the King is announced,
Even the King of Peace;
And they who are stricken and afflicted shall be made glad;
The mourners and they that sorrow shall look up, and rejoice:
The chains of them that are bound shall be broken, and they shall
go free;
The defiled shall be cleansed and purified,
And the weary and travel-stained shall be at rest.
Come, ye that are thirsty, and drink ;
Come, ye that hunger, and be filled;
For the Water of Immortality is found,
And the Bread of Life is made known.
Awake, ye sleepers, and shake off the dreams of illusion !
Rouse ye from the stupor of mortality !
And slumber no more in the realm of self !
For the Master of Compassion is revealed,
The Law of Good is expounded,
And the Great Reality of a stainless life is accomplished !
The Truth of the ages is made plain;
In the tabernacle of the holy heart it is revealed.
The guileless perceive it;
The righteous hear it;
The holy realise it.
It is manifested in all its glory in the conqueror of sin.
Ye that search in the darkness,
Come now unto the Light;
Ye that see the evil and the woe without,
Come with me, and I will show you its source:–

Go ye into the secret chambers of your hearts,
Seek there until ye find ;
Meditate there until ye awake.
He that dreams in self is asleep in Truth.
The dreamer can neither know himself nor the awakened ;
The awakened knoweth both himself and the dreamer,
He also knoweth the emptiness of the thing dreamed.
The sleeper in self is involved in evil ;
He is encompassed with darkness;
He is surrounded with woe ;
Such is the plight of the dreamer,
And the source, continuance, and end of evil are hidden from him.
Awake ! therefore, ye that sleep !
Awake from the sleep of lust !
Awake from the slumber of hatred !
Come out of the painful dreams of avarice, self-indulgence, vanity and pride !
Shake off the nightmare of doubt!
Be drugged no more by groundless faith,
By error, and the clinging unto death !
End ye the sleep of self, and awake in the Reality of Truth !
For the end of self is the beginning of Truth. Behold, the glorious Truth !
Awake ! awake ! awake ! ye are sleeping I ye
are dreaming ! Awake! Sons of the Morning, and fill the world with music.
Come ye, and dwell in the Light;
Come ye, and tread the Path of Perfection ;
Come ye, and be exalted with the exaltation of Holiness,
So shall ye. know the supreme Love and Peace.

The Second Prophecy, called the Messiah

CONSIDER the signs of the times:
War is rampant, strife is raging,
And the fires of passion are devastating the earth ;
Nation is opposed to nation, creed to creed and system to system :
Science has discovered its own weakness,

47

Philosophy has confounded philosophy,
And a confusion of mental tongues has become universal.
Yet in the height of all this confusion,
In the midst of the fierce clash of prejudice and passion,
One has descended whose name is Love,
Whose mission is Peace,
And whose end is Unity.
Walking in the midst is He,
But men know Him not because of their infirmities ;
Yet at His touch the blind receive their sight,
The deaf hear, and the lame walk.
Silently, holily is He working in isolated hearts:
Here and there a disciple is called,
And he hears and follows;
And the disciple knows his Master, and the Master His disciple.
The Chosen Few have not been deaf to the command, "Follow Me",
And they have followed with sure and certain steps.
They have gazed upon the face of the Serene One ;
They have sat at the feet of the Perfect One;
They have accepted the instruction of the Holy One,
And peace abides with them.
They walk amongst men, and are not discerned ;
They have relinquished all strife in their inmost hearts,
Hating none, condemning none ;
They have entered the Gate of Forgiveness;
Goodwill is the breath of their nostrils,
And boundless charity is the master of their
thoughts. They have ceased from vain longings ;
They have chased away all fluctuating desires;
They have passed through the Gate of Sacrifice,
They have clothed themselves with the Garment of Humility,
They tread the Path of Good, and their gait is steadfast.
Fear and doubt they have dispersed ;
They walk upon the turbulent waters of sorrow,
And they sink not, and are comforted.
They are no longer confounded by false philosophy ;
They have passed through the Sea and the Desert,
And have entered the Promised Land.

And these are they who have been born again for the salvation of
the world ;
In the time of darkness, they have accepted the Light;
In the time of evil, they have chosen the Good;
In the day of self-seeking, they have silenced the many voices of
self,
And have followed the One Voice whose music harmonises all.
Therefore, they rejoice;
Not blind to the evil,
But because the Omniscient One has shown them the end of evil;
Yea, in themselves they have already accomplished that end,
For they have become One with Him whom they have followed.
All that belongs to the world they have given to the world,
And they have not murmured.
The clouds of confusion do not darken them,
And the fires of passion do not scorch them;
Therefore let gladness reign !
For with the great darkness of these times, there has also come
great Light ;
Though the rivers of sorrow are swollen high,
The banks are perfumed with the flowers of blessedness ;
Though strife is raging, Peace has entered into the midst ;
Though confusion has covered the earth, unity has been revealed ;
And though many continue to dream the dreams of illusion,
The vision of the Great Reality has gladdened the ken of the
wakeful.
Awake, ye sleepers! Arouse yourselves, ye dreamers !
When will ye open your eyes, and see ?
The Perfect One has appeared!
The stainless majesty of the Holy One is revealed ;
His sleepless watchers have hailed Him,
And He has borne away their weariness.
Come, then, ye sorrowing, and be glad !
Come, ye weary, and find peace !
Come, ye toilers, and be at rest !
For the longing of the ages is fulfilled,
And He whom we call Master has appeared :–
He is the sacred inmost heart of Love.

The Third prophecy, called the All - One

TO do good and to remain unknown,
Let this be called Humility ;
To bless one's persecutors,
Let this be called Love ;
To rejoice at the good fortune of one's enemies,
Let this be called Perfection :
Thus is the All-One manifested,
Thus is the Truth made known.
The knowers of the All-One are perfect ;
They are without sin,
Dwelling in Truth and robed with holiness.
Behold ! the All-One is revealed,
He is made known to His worshippers ;
The garment of evil has fallen away from them,
And they have put on the perfect garment of Good;
The old bottles of error are broken,
And the new bottles of Truth are filled with the Wine of Life.
The believers in the-All-One drink and are satisfied.
And the doers of His word enter into the joy of immortality.
And who are they that believe in the All-One?
Who are the doers of His Word ?
The believer and doer is known by these sure signs,–
He is freed from ignorance and is not enslaved by likes and
dislikes ;
He is freed from hatred, and does not condemn ;
He is freed from partiality, and does not engage in strife ;
He is freed from self-seeking, and does not defend himself.
He never lets go of patience ;
He does not doff the robe of Purity;
He goes not out from the dwelling-place of Love.
The knower of the All-One is perfect in knowledge.
He is blameless in thought, word, and deed.
The All-One is sought by practice,
He is perceived by knowledge,
And he is realised by the perfection of practice and the
consummation of knowledge.

To rise above good and evil,
Hatred and love,
Prejudice and error,
Desire and pain,
Self - love and sorrow,
Passion and remorse,
Life and death,
Is to enter the unending peace of the All-One,
Is to realise the immortality of the All-One,
Is to become the All-One.
The All - One is that Perfect Good which is beyond both good and
evil;
He is that Perfect Love which neutralises love and hate;
He is that Perfect Life which is not broken by life and death.
He that would know Him, let him become His disciple.
Let him remove the ever - changing opposites within until he
comes to that which changes not;
So shall he find the Eternal Rock,
Even the blessed All-One, the Master of peace.
He that searches without, he shall not find ;
He that is proud of his knowledge, he shall not find;
He that fortifies himself against others, he shall not find ;
Realise, O disciple! thine inward error,
Thine inward ignorance,
Thine inward delusion rooted in self ;
And, having realised, leave error and cling to Truth;
Fly from ignorance to the knowledge that is pure.
And fortify thyself against the enemies within thyself.
By this way is the All-One approached,
By none other is He accessible;
He that is willing to be naked to self, let him come and be clothed
with Truth ;
He that is willing to die to error, let him come and be reborn as a
child of Truth;
He that is willing to become empty, let him come and be filled
with the knowledge of the All - One.
The Good that is supreme,
The Humility that is sublime,
The love that transcends all sorrow,–

To this attainment shall he surely come
Who seeks the All-One by the Path of Peace.

The Fourth Prophecy, called Unrest

HE voice of the Spirit to the children of the flesh,–
This is darkness,–to be enslaved by sin ;
This is light,–to be free from sin.
There is a place of darkness,
A dwelling - place of deep darkness,
And they who abide there cry out of their unrest,
They cry and are not heard, because their cry is of self;
They call upon their God, but the silence is not broken ;
The echo of their own voice they hear, and it affrights them.
And they remain in their sins.
And remaining in their sins, they shall cry,–
"We have sown wheat and have reaped straw,
We have ploughed, but we have no produce of our labour,
And lo ! the Great Famine is upon us.
We stored away much grain, but the rats have devoured it;
We put away much fruit, but it has decayed, and the long winter is
before us ;
We bartered, and acquired much gold, yet we perish,
For some the thief has stolen, and the rest is mouldy.
What shall we purchase, having no Bread?
There is no Bread, and no seller of Bread ;
We die, and there is none to save us !"
And again, in their deep bitterness, they shall say,–
"We have toiled mightily, but we have no reward;
That which we built is destroyed,
That which we made secure is undermined,
And all our wonderful works are crumbling away.
We ate and slept, but now we are afflicted,
We made sacrifices, yet now we are deserted,
We built ourselves pleasant mansions, and there is no rest in them.
Our sorrows are as the deep seas,
Our miseries are as the great mountains,
Our woes are many, and our pains are great.

There is no cure for our diseases,
There is no relief for our sorrows,
We are weary, and there is no rest !"
So shall they cry, and they shall not be heard;
So shall they suffer, and shall not be relieved ;
And they shall seek for rest, and shall not find it ;
For in the place of darkness,
In the dwelling-place of deep darkness,
There is no remedy,
There is no redress,
There is no salvation.
Where self is lord and king there is no peace.
Ye who are in the way of impurity,
Ye who are the subjects of self,
Listen, though ye understand not.
Hear,–for the day cometh when the precepts of the prophet are remembered,
And his words are burnt into the heart with brands of fire,–
Where there shall come upon you the night which is more than darkness,
The hunger which is more than famine,
And the deprivation which is more than death,
When Love shall be crucified, and hatred be set free,
When peace shall be banished, and strife be glorified.
When righteousness shall be mocked, and confusion shall flourish,
And the voice of the prophet is no longer heard;–
When that time comes, and ye cry, and are not heard,
Suffer, and are not relieved,
Sorrow, and are not comforted,
Remember this,–
He that rouseth himself early seeth the sun rise,
He that watcheth diligently and taketh a light, findeth his way out of the darkness,
And he that striveth with an uncomplaining heart, is crowned with the Crown of Peace.

The Fifth Prophecy, called Transition

THE Voice of the Spirit to the children of sorrow,—
Arise ye ! Awake !
Open your eyes, and see !
Why will ye sleep the sleep that is painful ?
Come out of the night of unrest,
Out of the dark nightmare of sin and affliction !
For there is a Way out of the place of darkness,
And out of the dwelling-place of deep darkness a Pathway that is
sure.
There shall be light and safety,
There shall be rest and healing,
There shall be joy and satisfaction.
There shall be no more dreaming for him who is awake,
Who says, with deep resolve, "I will abandon self, and Truth shall
be my Lord".
And thus resolving, there shall appear upon his right hand a
Gateway that is dark,
And upon his left hand a portal pleasant to behold ;
And he shall stoop and enter the Gateway that is dark,
And there shall come behind him mockeries and revilings, and
laughter that stingeth:
And, entering, he shall take up two swords.
The first is called the Sword of Searching,
And the second is called the Sword of Dividing;
And with the Sword of Searching he shall destroy the enemies of
Wisdom,
And with the Sword of Dividing he shall sever Good from evil.
He shall encounter all the enemies of Light;
Them that cast the Great Shadow he shall disperse,
And the strong keepers of the keys of hell he shall put to rout.
He shall pass through the Fire called Suffering and it shall not
devour him;
He shall cross the dark Ocean called Sorrow, and it shall not
swallow him up;
And when he cometh to the Great Desert called Desertion, he shall
not turn back.
And he shall come out of all his darkness,
He shall find the Shadowless Light.
Upon the outermost edge of the Great Darkness he shall hear a

Voice,
The Voice of the Holy One,
Then shall he know that the King of Truth is near,
And that there cometh the anointed Prince of Peace.
And he shall follow the Voice because it is gentle and true,
And it shall lead him to the eternal abode of Light,
Where every veil shall be lifted, and every mystery solved.
And he shall perceive the majesty of the Master of Truth ;
He shall behold the beauty of the Law of Righteousness ;
He shall gaze upon the glory of the Great Reality;
He shall hear the song of the redeemed,
Even this the sweet song of salvation :–
Sin is destroyed,
How perfect is the Law !
Sorrow is slain,
How mighty is Love !
The clouds of affliction are dispersed,
How glorious is the Light !
Error is fallen,
How immaculate is the Truth !
Awake ! ye sleepers,
Rejoice in the Truth !
Look up I ye fallen,
And rejoice in the Light !
Let the thirsty come and drink,
Let the hungry come and eat,
Let the dying come and live,
Salvation abounds, and redemption is sure.
And entering the Gate of Peace, the empires of this world shall be
to him as dust,
Its glories as clouds that are dispersed,
Its pleasures as chaff that is carried away,
And its pursuits as houses having no-foundation;
And the Voice of the Holy One shall say unto him,–
"Conqueror of self, Slayer of sin and sorrow,
Disperser of shadows and illusions,
Put away the Sword of Searching,
And let the Sword of Dividing be sheathed;
Here are no sorrows,

Here is no darkness and affliction,
And strife and division cannot enter here.
Lowly doer of righteousness, thou hast found my Law,
Silent seeker of Truth, thou hast found my Peace,
Lover of meekness and Good, thou hast found Me;
Take up thy abode in my eternal Habitation,
Thy warfare is ended, and thy rest is achieved."

The Sixth Prophecy, called Peace

THE Voice of the Spirit to the children of Truth,–
Rejoice, and be glad I Yea, be filled with gladness !
For the Great Task is completed, and there is no more labour ;
The Long Journey is ended, and there is no more weariness ;
The days are numbered, and the Saviour has come.
There is peace upon the hills, and in the valleys a tumult of great joy,
For the Child who is Love and Wisdom is apprehended,
And the Kingdom which is Goodwill and Peace is proclaimed.
Sing, ye holy ones !
Ye pure and peaceful, let your voices be heard !
Truth is established, and righteousness reigneth.
There is joy for every sorrow,
This is oil for every wound,
And there is healing for every broken heart.
For the weary there is a rest that endureth,
For the wandering an eternal refuge,
And for the despairing and tempest-tossed a harbour of great gladness,
Fur there is sinlessness of heart.
Out of the dark places of self,
Beyond the uncertain valley of Transition,
Is found the peaceful Path of Holiness.
Upon the high Peaks of Purity,
Upon the Mountains of Righteousness,
Even upon the lofty Hills of Love,
There abideth eternal peace,
There awaiteth everlasting rest.

Whosoever will climb, let him come and see;
Whosoever will strive, let him come and know ;
Whosoever will overcome, let him come and enter in.
The darkness is dispersed,
The power of evil is destroyed,
And the wheel of Fate is broken.
The Light abideth in eternal glory,
The power of Good is supreme,
And Righteousness and Love have broken every bond.
Death is slain, for Life is known ;
Doubt is no more, for immortality is tasted;
Fear is cast out, for Perfect Love is revealed,
The King of Truth is near,
And He is Perfect Knowledge ;
The Lord of Life is at hand,
And He is Perfect Purity ;
The Saviour is here, and He is Perfect Love;
Therefore, peace abideth,
Yea, abideth for ever.
These things are made known to the righteous,
To the wise their glory is revealed,
And by the guileless alone are these three Perfections
comprehended ;
For he that is unholy knoweth only that which is unholy ;
He that is holy knoweth holy things.
Perfection cannot be distorted,–
Behold its beauty !
Righteousness cannot be broken,–
How faultless are its proportions!
Truth remains undisturbed,–
How incomparable is its calm !
And because of this, there is great rejoicing,
Because of this, there is holy gladness,
Because of this, there is unending peace.

The First Exhortation, concerning Purity

THE Purity that is stainless,
To this I exhort men ;
To the Purity of the Highest I point the Sons of Light.
I exhort also the children of error to the excellent Way of Purity ;
For out of Purity groweth Truth,
And they who seek it, seek the heavenly Light.
Ye who are bound, come now and be free ;
Say not, "I am helpless", ye who are enslaved,
For the way of emancipation is opened up,
Yea, even salvation knocketh at your door.
Will you choose liberty ?
Or will ye rather choose to be bound ?
In Purity there is freedom,
Understanding dwelleth in her Temple,
And joy, and Gladness, and Peace are her doorkeepers.
Come, then, and listen to the exhortation of Truth,
And, having listened, do that which is pure,
And doing that which is pure ye shall know the supreme
blessedness.
Not in thy acts alone shalt thou find Purity,
The Purity of the Highest is not confined to acts.
Not by cutting off thy acts shalt thou become pure,
But by cleansing the source of thy acts,
Even thy mind and heart,
For a pure mind cannot commit impure acts,
Neither can a stainless heart bring forth any unlovely thing.
What, then, defileth, and what maketh clean?
The unchaste thought,
The impure desire,
The selfish inclination,
This defileth, and bringeth forth darkness and death.
The pure thought,
The holy aspiration,
The unselfish love,
This cleanseth, and bringeth forth Light and Life.
Come, then, and see how straight is the narrow Path of Purity !
Come and know how open and unsecret are the beautiful Courts of
Truth !
Come and understand how simple is the excellent Law of

Righeteousness!

Easy to find and pleasant to walk: is the path, of Purity ;
Open wide, and inviting entrance, are the Gates of Truth ;
Near at hand and ready for investigation is the Law of
Righteousness.

To harbour hateful thoughts,
To cherish lustful inclinations.
To nurture the seeds of malice in the heart,–
This defileth, and leadeth to suffering.
To thirst for pleasures and rewards,
To dwell upon the sins of others,
And to think, " I am better than this man,"–
This maketh impure and causeth thee to wander from Truth.
To seek for thyself and not to consider others,
To depreciate others, and to think highly of thine own Works,
And to make proud and stubborn thy heart,–
This staineth thy soul, and taketh thee away from thy peace.
Behold how glorious is the Path of Purity !
How lovely is the treasury of Truth !
How comely and beautiful is the Garment of Holiness !
To be free from hatred, lust and malice,–
How sweet ! How pleasant !
Not to desire pleasures and rewards,–
How good ! How joyful !
Not to magnify evil in others,–
How fair ! How lovely !
To put away all egotism,–
How beautiful! How peaceful !
The blessedness of a pure heart is beyond conception;
The loveliness of a sinless mind is beyond comparison ;
And supremely blissful is the immortality of the righteous.
Peace-producing is the Purity of the Highest;
Joy - inspiring is the stainlest life,
And rich in wisdom is the heat that is sinless.
Ye who are tired of sin ;
Ye who know the bitterness of impurity;
Ye who seek the everlasting peace,
Come and enter the door of Purity And let Holiness be your
companion.

Purify your thoughts ;
Wash white the garment of your mind ;
Cleanse ye the secret places of your heart :–
This done, Truth shall come and dwell with You;
Knowledge shall be your lamp, and wisdom your guide ;
Righteousness shall be your everlasting protection,
And Light, and Joy, and Peace shall abide with you for ever.

The Second Exhortation, concerning Humility

THE Humility that is blameless,
To this I exhort men ;
I point them to the sublime pathway of Humility.
Without Humility who shall see Truth?
Without Meekness who shall comprehend the All - One ?
Without Lowliness who shall find the Great Reality ?
Love dwelleth with Humility,
Wisdom also abideth there ;
And peace remaineth with the lowly heart.
Put away thy Pride,
Think no more of thy superiority,
And purge thy mind of all its vanity ;
Then shall the Truth dignify thee.
Truth fleeth from pride ;
Wisdom departeth from egotism ;
And holiness and vanity cannot dwell together.
Out of Humility cometh Light,
But darkness dwells with vanity and pride.
Of what art thou proud ? O man ! of thy beauty ?
Corruption awaits it.
Of thy garments ?
The moth and the dust shall destroy them.
Of thy possessions ?
To - morrow another shall possess them.
Of thy talents ?
Their lusture shall be dimmed.
Of thy fame ?
It shall disappear as a mist Of thy learning ?

Even now it is surpassed.
Of thy! works ?
They shall vanish away for ever.
What, then, remaineth, if these things are as naught ?
Wisdom remaineth, and Truth and Love ;
And Joy and Peace and Enlightenment are established.
But these cannot be known to the proud.
Neither can the vain man understand them,
And their glory is not revealed, to him that is subject to self.
What can darkness reveal ?
And he who walketh in darkness, what shall he see ?
The proud are blinded by darkness;
The vain stumble and lose their way ;
And grief and desolation are the end of self.
The enlightenment of Humility is more than learning ;
The power of Meekness is more than the strength of many
conquerors,
And he who makes lowly his mind establishes himself upon a rock.
How shall the proud stand ?
They fall of their own weakness.
How shall the vain endure ?
They are as reeds without support.
How shall the self-seeking flourish ?
They are as barren seed blown about and finding no soil.
Put on the Garment of Humility, and thou shalt not fall ;
Make gentle thy heart, and thou shalt endure as the mountain;
Put away self, and thy works shall flourish is seed upon good soil.
The arrogant regard themselves as kings, But they are less than
serfs;
The meek regard themselves as serfs,
But they are more than kings,
How easily are the proud injured,
Every day they suffer pain ;
How often arc the vain wounded.
Weeping and sorrow are their portion ;
How readily do the selfish suffer deprivation,
Every day they grieve over that they have lost.
There is no pain in Humility,
Meekness destroyeth sorrow,

And the pure in heart can suffer no loss.
What can a man retain ?
What endureth ?
And where dwelleth immortality ?
The things of the world pass away, and none can hold them ;
The body perishes, and is no more seen ;
And the opinions of men are as smoke in a high wind.
Holiness can be retained,
Truth endureth,
And immortality dwelleth in the sinless heart.
I sought the world, but peace was not there ;
I courted learning, but Truth was not revealed
I sojourned with philosophy, but my heart was sore with vanity
And I cried, " where is peace to be found ?
And where is the hiding - place of Truth ?"
In Humility I found peace,
In the practice of righteousness Truth was. revealed ;
And in self - obliteration I reached the end of pain and vanity.
Bend low, Ye pilgrims;
Prostrate Yourselves, Ye weary and disconsolate;
Give up that ye love, ye stricken and afflicted;
For he that bendeth himself shall be straightened,
He that prostrateth himself shall be lifted up,
And whosoever relinquishes self shall see the end of his afflictions.
Narrow and Low is the Portal of Humility,
But he that stoopeth, and entereth therein, shall stand for ever.

The Third Exhortation, concerning Love

THE Love that is perfect,
To this I exhort men ;
Even to the Love of the Highest.
How beautiful to behold is Love!
How glorious to contemplate !
And in practice how sweet and full of gladness!
To find Love is to find Perfection;
To know Love is to know the Eternal;
To practise Love is to manifest Truth.

But how is Love found ?
How is it revealed in the heart ?
How is it practised and made manifest?
Not to be a partisan,
Not to practise hatred,
Not to engage in strife,
Not to practise deception,
Not to covet,
Not to retaliate,
Not to condemn,–
Not to do all these is to find Love.
To put away prejudice,
To rid the mind of pride and vanity,
To disperse doubt and fear,
To wash from the heart the stains of desire.
To purify the mind of every defilement,–
To do all these is to know Love.
To be always patient,
To be supremely calm,
To be ceaselessly holy,
To be forgiving to the uttermost,
And to be equal - minded towards enemies as towards friends,–
To be all these is to manifest Love.
Where Love is, Light is,
Where Love is not, there is impenetrable darkness.
Where Love is, Life is ;
Where Love is not, there is the deeper death.
Where Love is, Truth is ;
Where Love is not, there is error and confusion
Love changes not, for Love is Truth ;
Love sins not, for Love is perfect;
Love grieves not, for Love is the Eternal;
Love is not subject to birth and death, for Love is Immortality.
How illusory is the world!
How fleeting and empty are the pleasures of the world !
How real is Love!
How steadfast and full of peace is the life of Truth!
How vain are the pursuits of men!
How heavy is the weariness of self !

But the practice of righteousness is fruitful.
And sweet is the peace of Truth.
He who hath Love hath all things,
The Master dwelleth in Love,
In Love the Great Reality abides,
And the wonderful Peace is only found by Love.
The Purity of the Highest is there,
The majesty of humility also,
And he who adjusts his heart to Love is perfect
Seek self, and Love shall be withheld from you;
Seek Love, and lo! it is already with you.
Who seeketh enlightenment ?
Who seeketh Truth ?
Who seeketh Love ?
Let him that seeketh, come, and say,–
" Open ! ye doors of Purity !
Be closed no more, ye narrow portals of Humility!
Swing open wide, ye everlasting gates of Love !
And his voice shall be heard in the innermost places:
He shall not cry in vain, nor shall he lose his way.
But shall pass through to his everlasting rest.

Instruction, concerning the Master

TO the obedient and the ready ;
To all who are willing to understand ;
To those wandering in the darkness, and: unable to perceive the
Light: –
Come now, and listen ;
Come now, and be made glad;
Enter now into the revelation of Purity.–
The Master is not perceived by the senses,
Not comprehended by the reason,
Not realised by argument.
Not on the hills, nor in the valleys ;
Not in the earth, nor sky, not in any outward thing is the Master to
be found.
Creeds and schools and books cannot contain Him,

He dwelleth within.
Cease from thine outward search, O weary one!
Cease from thy wanderings, O child of night !
In thine own heart dwelleth the Master ;
He is not hidden from thee but by thyself.
The Master is the inward Voice,
The inward Light,
The inward Peace.
Behold I show you the dwelling - place of the Master,–
It is a purified heart,
He who hath broken the bonds of self,
Who hath slain desire,
Whose mind is quiet, conquered, and subdued,
Whose heart is calm and mild and full of peace,
He hath entered the presence df the Master,
Unto him the glory of the Master is revealed.
O thou who criest and receivest no answer !
O thou who wanderest and findest no rest !
O thou who searchest and findest no Light !
Bring hither thy fainting heart,
Bring hither thy blindness,
Come and listen to the instruction that is holy,
And, having listened, find satisfaction and rest.–
There are truths many, and there is one Truth,
Even the pure mind, the supremely Perfect Life:
There are saviours many, and there is one Saviour,
Even the supreme enlightenment of Wisdom:-
There are teachers many and there is one Teacher,
Even the glorious revelation of Righteousness:
There are masters many, and there is one Master,
Even the Spirit of Truth;
And Truth, Saviour, Teacher and Master are one.
Plain and unmistakable is the way which leadeth to the Master,–
Overcome thyself, this is the Way.
Purify thy heart, and thou shalt gaze upon the face of the Master.
Cling to self, and thou shalt not find Him;
Abandon self arid lo ! the Master abideth with thee.
The impure have no eyes to see the pure,
The darkness cannot penetrate the Light,

And immortality is hidden from that which is perishable.
Therefore, leave that to which thou clingest.
Yield up thy desires,
And the satisfaction of the Master shall fil thee.
Yield up thy opinions,
And the Light of the Master shall illumine thee;
Go not after the evanescent and the perishable,
And thou shalt enter into the possession of the Eternal and
imperishable ;
Thou shalt become one with the Master,
And shalt dwell with Him in Immortality,
The Master waiteth,
Yea, eternally waiteth,
Patience is His name;
He departeth not from compassion,
And where Righteousness abides, there dwelleth He.
Hidden is He in Love ;
Come unto Love, and thou shalt find Him.
The Light of Wisdom envelopeth Him ;
Purify thine understanding, and thou shalt know Him.
The glory of Truth covereth Him up;
Relinguish self, and thou shalt see His Form.
Why perceivest thou not the Truth?
Why hearest thou not the Voice of the Master?
Thou perceivest not the Truth because of thine own errors;
Thou hearest not the Master's Voice because the voices of self
clamour loudly within thee.
As clouds hide the face of the sun,
So the clouds of error hide the face of the Master;
Yea, the thick clouds of sin they shut Him but from men.
Who, then, shall see the Master?
Who shall comprehend Him ?
Who shall dwell with Him?
Who shall hear His Voice ?
Even he who is of a pure heart ;
Who is gentle, compassionate, and infinitely patient;
Who returneth meekness for anger,
Love for hatred,
Forgiveness for abuse,

And silence for condemnation.
Clothe thyself, therefore, in the Garment of Humility;
Acknowledge thine errors,
Even thine inmost sins,
Thus confessing thyself,
thou shalt find the Way of Love,
And finding Love thou shalt find the Master ;
And finding the Master thou shalt be at rest.
Deny thyself ;
Subdue thyself ;
Conquer thyself.
Let not goodwill depart from thee ;
Be at peace with all, yea, even with the beasts,
So shall the highest Truth take up its abode within thee ;
Unto thee the heart of the Master shall be revealed;
Sorrow and suffering and fear and doubt shall flee far from thee,
And the knowledge of immortality shall fill thy heart with peace.
Thus is the heart of the Master made known,
Thus is He revealed unto them that are ready to receive Him.

Instruction, concerning the Law

TO the humble and the faithful ;
To them that are seeking humility and faith,–
There is one Supreme Law,
Even the Law of Good.
Think not that which is evil;
Say not that which is evil ;
Do not that which is evil,
Think that which is good ;
Say that which is good;
Do that which is good,
So shalt thou come to know the Law ;
By no other way can it be comprehended.
The knowledge of the Law maketh the heart glad,
It filleth the mind with joy,
It destroyeth all sorrow.
Suffering ceases for him who knows the Law,

Sin and grief and affliction leave him,
And wheresoever he goes, peace follows him.
Happy is he who has perceived the Law;
Blessed is he who practises it;
Divine is he who has become one with it.
Come, thou that searchest, weary and almost hopeless,
Prostrate thyself in the dust of obedience;
Deny thyself to the uttermost ;
Leave all that thou art proud of;
Yea, sacrifice all ;
So shalt thou put on the yoke of Lowliness,
And shalt thou enter into a knowledge of the Law;
Then shalt thou come to know the three Names of the Law of
Good,–
The first is Justice;
The second, Righteousness;
The third, Love.
Men, loving self, deny these lofty names,
And have no knowledge of the Law of Good;
Wandering in the dark, they fall into treacherous places,
And fear and doubt and sorrow and suffering dwell with them.
Practise the inward Righteousness,
And thou shalt see the ineffable glory of the three Names;
Thou shalt comprehend the Law of Good,
And bliss and peace shall fill thee.
To know the Law ;
To obey the Law ;
To practise the Law,–
This only is salvation,
This only is emancipation from error and unrest.
Supremely glorious is the Law of Good,
Supremely peace - giving is the knowledge of the Law,
Supremely blessed is he whose pilgrim feet walk in obedience to
the Law.
He who says,–
I will no more cling to self ;
I will no more engage in strife ;
I will no more retaliate ;
I will no more judge and condemn.

Hitherto I have clung to self;
I have sought to gratify self;
I have defended and protected myself;
But now I will abandon self;
I will sacrifice and not defend myself;
Yea, utmost crucifixion shall be mine.
I will love all men, and only myself will I condemn;
The Garment of Humility shall cover me;
Righteousness and Love shall be my protection;
Even in the Highest will I take my refuge.
Goodwill shall be my guide;
Compassion shall not depart from me.
And the divine gentleness of Truth shall guide my thoughts and actions.
Thus will I cease from sin;
Thus will I practise the Highest Good.
He who thus resolves shall know the Law,
The Law of Good shall he comprehend;
The fulness of its majesty shall be revealed to him,
And from all evil shall he be protected.
Therefore, let a man believe in Good;
Let him cling to Good;
Let him practise Good;
He will thus come to comprehend himself;
Comprehending himself he will comprehend the universe;
He will thus arrive at peace.
When a man's body is defiled, does he not wash it and make it clean?
When a man's heart is defiled, let him likewise wash it, and be clean.
Five are the waters which wash away sin:—
Purity, which washes away all indulgences and lusts;
Pity, which washes away all self-seeking and indifference;
Humility, which washes away all prejudice and pride;
Joy, which washes away all covetousness and envy;
Love, which washes away all hatred and condemnation.
Whosoever will, let him come and be clean,
The waters are ready and waiting.
Blessed he is who is free from sin.

He knows the supreme Law of Good, and dwells in peace.
Thus is the Law qf Good expounded ;
Thus is it spread abroad in the hearts of men.

Instruction, concerning The Great Reality

TO the awakened and enlightened,
To those who seek to be awakened and enlightened,–
There is darkness and there is Light ;
There is dreaming and there is Waking ;
There is illusion and there is Reality.
The darkness apprehendeth not the Light ;
The dreamer knoweth not his waking mind ;
And the wanderer in illusion is unacquainted with Reality ;
Of two ways, therefore, one must be abandoned.
The dweller in darkness seeth nothing,
Not even himself,
His feet stumble, he knoweth not his way.
Abandon darkness, and thou shalt come unto the Light;
Coming to the Light, thou shalt see all things:
Thou shalt know thy way, and thy feet shall cease from stumbling.
The way of the dreamer is uncertain and painful;
Pleasure and terror afflict him ;
He knoweth not where he standeth;
He controlleth not himself, and is at the mercy of the unreal.
Abandon the dreams of self, O thou that sleepest !
Awake ! open thine eyes to the Morning,
And thou shalt comprehend thine own divinity.
The walker in the way of illusion is surrounded with shadows;
He perceiveth not the substance ;
Grasping at bubbles, he is scourged with grief and disappointment;
Clinging to the perishable, he mourns,
And following after that which vanishes, he is troubled with unrest.
Abandon the pathway of illusion,
The pathway of thy perishable self,
So shalt thou find the imperishable Truth;
Gladness shall take the place of mourning,
And thine eyes shall be opened to the glory of the Great Reality.

What, then, is the Great Reality ?
The Great Reality is a stainless heart,
An enlightened understanding,
A soul whose perfect peace is not disturbed.
By the practice of righteousness only can the Great Reality be known ;
He alone can perceive it who controls himself;
He alone can enter it who purifies himself ;
He alone can abide therein who is free from all sin.
In the Great Reality all religions and philosophies culminate,
They meet here, and then vanish away,
For there is no division in the Great Reality,
Strife and unrest cannot enter there,
And he who comes to it is filled with peace.
Thou who wouldst understand the Great Reality ;
Thou who would'st enter it, and know its peace;
Seek the One behind the many,
Seek the Silence behind the noise,
Seek Truth behind self ;
Seek for that which is holy and peace-giving,
Which abides, and does not pass away like the morning dew.
Wisdom abides ;
Love abides ;
Compassion abides ;
Truth abides;
Therefore sacrifice self,
For self and all the things of self are perishable,
They belong to the unreal !
Awake, then, out of thy dreaming!
Disperse all thy shadows,
Destroy all thine illusions,
And thou shalt enter the Great Reality;
Filled with peace, thou shalt dwell with the Eternal Harmonies ;
Filled with bliss, thou shalt sing the everlasting Song,
The Song which thrills the spaces and the worlds ;
Thy Song and mine thus shalt thou sing,—
I have made the acquaintance of the Master of Compassion;
I have put on the Garment of the Perfect Law ;
I have entered the realm of the Great Reality.

Wandering is ended, for Rest is accomplished ;
Pain and sorrow have ceased, for Peace is entered into;
Confusion is dissolved, for Unity is made manifest;
Error is vanquished, for Truth is revealed.
Blessed is he who has resolved to abandon self:
Blessed is he who is pure;
Blessed is he who has destroyed all his illusions;
He has found the Great Reality at last.
The universe is glad, for again the Master is revealed;
The universe is glad, for again the Law of Good is expounded;
The universe is glad, for again the Great Reality is comprehended.

Discourse Concerning The Way of Truth

1. Self - Restraint

WHAT is Truth ?
It resides in the silence of Perfect Deeds.
That silence is sufficient for the wise.
I, therefore, discourse not upon Truth,
I discourse upon the Way which leads thither;
For Truth is not of words, but of life,
And though Truth govern the tongue, its seat is not there,
Its seat is in the heart.
What words shall add beauty to the ineffable?
And what man shall glorify Truth?
Let the ineffable give beauty to words,
And let man be glorified by Truth,
I, therefore, point the Way which leads to Truth.
Not by speculation do I point the Way,
But by practice and attainment:
The Way is named *Self - conquest.*
I write for believers,
For them that believe that self can be overcome.
I write not for them that deny that self can be overcome,
And who thus exalt and give dominion to self.

72

He who believes, will walk the holy Way,
And, walking it, will reach the highest Truth.
Let him who thus believes, equip himself :–
Helmeted with Faith, Armoured with Patience,
And armed with the sharp Sword of Resolution,
He will be prepared to attack the enemies of Truth within-himself;
He will enter upon the Practices of Truth.
By practice the artisan becomes accomplished in his craft,
By practice the Truth - lover becomes accomplished in Truth.
The Way of Truth is marked by three Great Practices,–
The first is Self - Restraint,
The second, Self - Examination,
The third, Self- Surrender ;
These three include all others,
He who refuses to practise Self - Restraint,
Who says in his heart, –
" I will eat and drink, and make me garlands of pleasure,"
He cannot find the Way which leads to peace.
But he who says within himself,–
" I will dwell with Abstinence,
I will make my abode with Chastity,
Integrity shall be my companion,
And faith shall light up my darkness,
Yea, Virtue shall be my refuge and my stay,"
He will find the Way which leads to Truth,
Lo! he hath already found it,
For the practice of virtue is the entrance to the Way.
The vicious man destroys, but the virtuous man builds ;
He slays himself who thinks only of his own pleasure;
He preserves himself who controls himself.
He who renounces pleasure, and restrains his passions,
Preferring steadfastness and integrity to gratification,
Will partake of the joys of virtue :
Pleasant will be his friendships,
Pure his affections,

And long and prosperous his days ;
Thus walking with virtue, happiness will wait upon him,
Partial blessedness will be his portion,
And he will reach the first great Resting-Place;
Yet, staying there, he will not reach the Highest.

2. Self-Examination

He who seeks the Highest will enter upon the practice of Self -
Examination.
Searching the inmost recesses of his heart,
Following up the intricate threads of thought,
Rigorously testing the quality of his motives,
He will find out the hidden springs of desire,
He will lay bare the roots of the tree of life,
And finding the Eternal Cause, he will know both Good and evil,
He will see the Highest, and will no more perish.
As a beautiful flower is formed, its growth not being seen,
So will he grow in wisdom, unseen of men.
Yet when wisdom is fully formed,
When the flower of Truth becomes manifest in all its beauty,
Men unacquainted with its silent growth will say.
"This man is wise, whence obtained he his wisdom ?
How knoweth this man letters, having never learned?"
As a child in the womb.
As a plant in the earth,
As an object in the eye of the approaching traveller,
So wisdom is formed in the heart,
So knowledge grows in him who diligently examines himself;
Who, having found the roots of evil,
Tears them up with the hands of Renunciation,
And burns them to ashes in the fire of Knowledge.
He who thus examines himself,
Who rectifies his inmost heart,
And rejects all the errors of his mind,
Who, seeking out and humbly acknowledging his own faults,
Refusing to dwell upon the faults of others,
Will make swift progress toward the goal of peace.

He will cleanse his heart ;
He will purify his understanding ;
Subduing self, he will no longer look through the eye of self;
Apprehending Truth, he will perceive with the unveiled eye of
Truth ;
He will know both self and Truth.
All his works will prosper, for his acts will be righteous ;
His tongue will speak wisdom, for his heart will be pure ;
And where his feet have trodden, the flowers of Love and Peace
will grow.
He will refuse to dwell with unrighteousness.
Folly and impurity he will reject,
And he will say unto strife and hatred, " Depart ye from me."
Kindling the fire of inward knowledge,
Keeping bright and constant its flame,
And feeding it with patient and loving sacrifice,
Let a man burn up all that is perishable within him,
Only thus will he find the Imperishable ;
Let him eliminate the dross of error,
Only thus will he discover the gold of Truth :
Let him destroy all sin, Only thus will he find the Stainless One,
Only thus will he approach the Highest.
Thus seeking out the source within himself.
Passion will not long torment him ;
Finding the cause of passion, he will destroy it,
And self - restraint will give way to composure of mind and heart,
Far will he travel on the Way of Peace,
And, reaching the second Resting - Place,
Will taste of fuller joy and blessedness.
Yet, staying there, he will not reach the Highest.

3. Self - Surrender

Having well restrained himself,
Having deeply examined himself,
Let the lover of Truth now enter upon the practice of Self -
Surrender.
He who practises self - restraint travels well;

He who practises self - examination travels better;
He who practises self - surrender travels best.
He only can know the Highest who surrenders self,
Who makes the inward sacrifice complete,
Who holds nothing back,
Who calls nothing his own,
Who refuses to set his heart upon any earthly thing ;
Putting aside all his lusts,
Emptying himself of all his vanities,
Divesting himself of all his theories and opinions,
He will become empty, naked, and without possessions ;
And having become empty, he will be filled with Truth ;
Having become naked, he will be clothed with Righteousness ;
Possessing nothing, he will be lord of all.
When self surrender is practised in its completeness.
Then is the Highest reached,
Then is Truth comprehened,
Then is Perfect Peace enjoyed.
He who has conquered himself can never be brought low,
He who has surrendered himself can never be confounded;
He who has overcome the world can never be disturbed,
The flames of lust will not burn him, for he has quenched them ;
Temptation will no more scourge him, for he has destroyed the
cause of temptation ;
Restraint will no more be needed, for he will be perfect in Truth,
Freed from self, he will be freed from sorrow;
Freed from error, he will no more grieve ;
Freed from impurity, he will cease from suffering.
He will enter into the highest joy,
And, reaching the final Resting - Place,
Will partake of perfect bliss and blessedness.
Not valuing that which perishes he can never be robbed;
Not loving himself he can never be wounded ;
And though men should slay him he can never be destroyed;
For he is no longer self, but Truth,
And who shall destroy Truth ?
All bodies die, but Truth does not die ;
Ail things pass away, but Truth remains for ever.
He who has surrendered self has become, immortal,

He is no longer separate but has become one with Truth,
And he manifests the Highest, though men perceive it not.
Of self - restraint is born Virtue,
Of self - examination is born Knowledge,
Of self - surrender is born Love.
Happy shall he become who restrains himself,
Blessed shall he become who purifies himself,
Divine shall he become who surrenders himself.
By Virtue one's life is governed,
By Knowledge one's life is purified,
By Love one's life is perfected.
Virtue is the seed, Knowledge the plant, and Love the flower.
The seed knoweth not the plant,
The plant knoweth not the flower,
But the flower knoweth itself, plant, and seed.
By self-restraint passion is slain ;
By self - examination false belief is slain;
By self - surrender all illusion is laid low.
Self - restraint leads to strength ;
Self - examination leads to wisdom;
Self-surrender leads to holiness.
Perfect in self-restraint, self-examination and self - surrender.
A man has reached the Highest;
He has become one with Truth, and will no more wander.
Unalterable in compassion,
Firmly established in righteousness,
And steadfast in holiness,
His heart thrills in unison with the Heart of all;
He knows the unending joy,
He has found the heavenly peace.
Having stooped to the lowest, he is exalted to the Highest;
Having conquered sin, he is crowned with Holiness ;
Having crucified self, he is glorified by Truth.
Willing to be nothing, he has become all ;
Yielding up all things, he has become possessed of all;
Giving his life, he is clothed with Immortality.
Altogether virtuous, he is altogether happy ;
Altogether righteousness, he is altogether blessed ;
Altogether pure, he is altogether peaceful.

Beautiful in Meekness,
Majestic in Love,
And invincible in Innocence,
He will manifest the Ineffable ;
He will teach without words.
No more troubled ;
No more tormented ;
No more afflicted;
Arisen, awakened, healed, and made perfect;
He has unveiled the Face of the Highest ;
He knows the Great Rest,
The Deep Silence,
The Profound Peace.
In the Light which knows no darkness he walks,
And it casts no shadow on his pathway.

Made in the USA
Middletown, DE
27 December 2015